W9-ADI-931

Problem Solving, Communication, and Reasoning

Spatial Sense

grade
1

Carole Greenes
Linda Schulman Dacey
Rika Spungin

Dale Seymour Publications®
White Plains, New York

DALE SEYMOUR PUBLICATIONS®

This book is published by Dale Seymour Publications®,
an imprint of Addison Wesley Longman, Inc.

Dale Seymour Publications
10 Bank Street
White Plains, New York 10602
Customer Service: 800-872-1100

Managing Editor: Catherine Anderson
Senior Editor: John Nelson
Project Editor: Mali Apple
Production/Manufacturing Director: Janet Yearian
Sr. Production/Manufacturing Coordinator: Fiona Santoianni
Design Director: Phyllis Aycock
Cover and Interior Illustrations: Jared Lee
Text and Cover Design: Tracey Munz
Composition and Line Art: Alan Noyes

Order number 21872
ISBN 0-7690-0014-2

1 2 3 4 5 6 7 8 9 10-ML-02 01 00 99 98

This Book Is Printed
On Recycled Paper

Contents

Introduction

Why Was *Hot Math Topics* Developed?

The *Hot Math Topics* series was developed for several reasons:

- to offer children practice and maintenance of previously learned skills and concepts
- to enhance problem solving and mathematical reasoning abilities
- to build literacy skills
- to nurture collaborative learning behaviors

Practicing and maintaining concepts and skills

Although textbooks and core curriculum materials do treat the topics explored in this series, their treatment is often limited by the lesson format and the page size. As a consequence, there are often not enough opportunities for children to practice newly acquired concepts and skills related to the topics, or to connect the topics to other content areas. *Hot Math Topics* provides the necessary practice and mathematical connections.

Similarly, core instructional programs often do not do a very good job of helping children maintain their skills. Although textbooks do include reviews of previously learned material, they are frequently limited to sidebars or boxed-off areas on one or two pages in each chapter, with four or five exercises in each box. Each set of problems is intended only as a sampling of previously taught topics, rather than as a complete review. In the selection and placement of the review exercises, little or no attention is given to levels of complexity of the problems. By contrast, *Hot Math Topics* targets specific topics and gives children more experience with concepts and skills related to them. The problems are sequenced by difficulty, allowing children to hone their skills. And, because they are not tied to specific lessons, the problems can be used at any time.

Enhancing problem solving and mathematical reasoning abilities

Hot Math Topics presents children with situations in which they may use a variety of problem solving strategies, including

- designing and conducting experiments to generate or collect data
- guessing, checking, and revising guesses
- organizing data in lists or tables in order to identify patterns and relationships
- choosing appropriate computational algorithms and deciding on a sequence of computations
- using inverse operations in "work backward" solution paths

For their solutions, children are also required to bring to bear various methods of reasoning, including

- deductive reasoning
- inductive reasoning
- proportional reasoning

For example, to solve clue-type problems, children must reason deductively and make inferences about mathematical relationships in order to generate candidates for the solutions and to home in on those that meet all of the problem's conditions.

To identify and continue a pattern and then write a rule for finding the next term in that pattern, children must reason inductively.

To estimate measures by comparing a smaller object to a larger object, children have to reason proportionally.

Building communication and literacy skills

Hot Math Topics offers children opportunities to write and talk about mathematical ideas. For many problems, children must describe their solution paths, justify their solutions, give their opinions, or write or tell stories.

Some problems have multiple solution methods. With these problems, children may have to compare their methods with those of their peers and talk about how their approaches are alike and different.

Other problems have multiple solutions, requiring children to confer to be sure they have found all possible answers.

Finally, spatial sense problems offer children opportunities to apply vocabulary related to position.

Nurturing collaborative learning behaviors

Several of the problems can be solved by children working together. Some are designed specifically as partner problems. By working collaboratively, children can develop expertise in posing questions that call for clarification or verification, brainstorming solution strategies, and following another person's line of reasoning.

What Is in *Spatial Sense*?

This book contains 100 problems and tasks that focus on ideas related to spatial sense. The mathematics content, the mathematical connections, the problem solving strategies, and the communication skills that are emphasized are described below.

Mathematics content

Spatial sense problems and tasks require children to

- estimate, measure, compare, and order lengths
- estimate and compare area and volume
- use positional terms
- describe, draw, identify, and build shapes
- identify attributes of shapes
- compare figures for similarities and differences
- use ordinal numbers
- predict the effect of changes in position and compare shapes in various positions
- determine figure-ground relationships
- identify symmetry
- recognize congruent figures
- identify shapes in real-world situations

Mathematical connections

In these problems and tasks, connections are made to these other topic areas:

- number sense
- graphs
- fractions

Problem solving strategies

Spatial Sense problems and tasks offer children opportunities to use one or more of several problem solving strategies.

- **Formulate Questions and Stories:** When data are presented in displays or text form, children must pose one or more questions that can be answered using the given data or create stories using the data.

- **Complete Stories:** When confronted with an incomplete story, children must supply the missing information and then check that the story makes sense.

- **Organize Information:** To ensure that several solution candidates for a problem are considered, children may have to organize information by drawing a picture or making a list.

- **Guess, Check, and Revise:** In some problems, children have to identify or generate candidates for the solution and then check whether those candidates match the conditions of the problem. If the conditions are not satisfied, other possible solutions must be generated and verified.

- **Identify and Continue Patterns:** To identify the next term or terms in a sequence, children have to recognize the relationship between successive terms and then generalize that relationship.

- **Use Logic:** Children have to reason deductively, from clues, to make inferences about the solution to a problem. They have to reason inductively to continue patterns.

Communication skills

Problems and tasks in *Spatial Sense* are designed to stimulate communication. As part of the solution process, children may have to

- describe their thinking steps
- describe patterns and rules
- find alternate solution methods and solution paths
- identify other possible answers
- give directions to classmates
- formulate problems for classmates to solve
- compare estimates, solutions, and methods with classmates
- make drawings to clarify mathematical relationships

These communication skills are enhanced when children interact with one another and with the teacher. By communicating both orally and in writing, children develop their understanding and use of the language of mathematics.

How Can *Hot Math Topics* Be Used?

The problems may be used as practice of newly learned concepts and skills, as maintenance of previously learned ideas, and as enrichment experiences for early finishers or more advanced students.

They may be used in class or given to children to take home and do with their families. If used during class, they may be selected to complement lessons dealing with a specific topic or assigned every week as a means of keeping skills alive and well.

For children whom the reading require-ments of the problems exceed their current abilities, you may wish to use the problems in whole-class or group settings, where either you or an able reader presents the problems aloud.

As they become more able readers, children can work on the problems in pairs or on their own. The problems are sequenced from least to most difficult. The selection of problems may be made by the teacher or the children based on their needs or interests. If the plan is for children to choose problems, you may wish to copy individual problems onto card stock and laminate them, and establish a problem card file.

To facilitate record keeping, a Management Chart is provided on page 6. The chart can be duplicated so that there is one for each child. As a problem is completed, the space corresponding to that problem's number may be shaded. An Award Certificate is included on page 6 as well.

How Can Children's Performance Be Assessed?

Spatial Sense problems and tasks provide you with opportunities to assess children's

- knowledge of geometry, measurement, and spatial relationships
- problem solving abilities
- mathematical reasoning methods
- communication skills

Observations

Keeping anecdotal records helps you to remember important information you gain as you observe children at work. To make observations more manageable, limit each observation to a group of from four to six children or to one of the areas noted above. You may find that using index cards facili-tates the recording process.

Discussions

Many of the *Spatial Sense* problems and tasks allow for multiple answers or may be solved in a variety of ways. This built-in richness motivates children to discuss their work with one another. Small groups or class discussions are appropriate. As children share their approaches to the problems, you will gain additional insights into their content knowledge, mathematical reasoning, and communication abilities.

Scoring responses

You may wish to holistically score children's responses to the problems and tasks. The simple scoring rubric below uses three levels: high, medium, and low.

High	Medium	Low
• Solution demonstrates that the child knows the concepts and skills.	• Solution demonstrates that the child has some knowledge of the concepts and skills.	• Solution shows that the child has little or no grasp of the concepts and skills.
• Solution is complete and thorough.	• Solution is complete.	• Solution is incomplete or contains major errors.
• The child communicates effectively.	• The child communicates somewhat clearly.	• The child does not communicate effectively.

Portfolios

Having children store their responses to the problems in *Hot Math Topics* portfolios allows them to see improvement in their work over time. You may want to have them choose examples of their best responses for inclusion in their permanent portfolios, accompanied by explanations as to why each was chosen.

Children and the assessment process

Involving children in the assessment process is central to the development of their abilities to reflect on their own work, to understand the assessment standards to which they are held accountable, and to take ownership for their own learning. Young children may find the reflective process difficult, but with your coaching, they can develop such skills.

Discussion may be needed to help children better understand your standards for performance. Ask children such questions as, "What does it mean to communicate *clearly*?" "What is a *complete* response?" Some children may want to use simple icons to score their responses, such as these characters:

What Additional Materials Are Needed?

Some manipulative materials are required for solving the problems in *Spatial Sense*, including cubes; tangrams; color tiles; pattern blocks; geometric solids; Cuisenaire® rods; interlocking cubes (such as Multilink™ cubes), 5-by-5 dot grids or square geoboards with rubber bands; graph paper; a mirror; a spoon, a paper cup, and beans; paper clips; and toothpicks. Crayons, colored pencils, tracing paper, and scissors should be readily accessible.

Management Chart

Name _____

When a problem or task is completed, shade the box with that number.

1	2	3	4	5	6	7	8	9	10
11	12	13	14	15	16	17	18	19	20
21	22	23	24	25	26	27	28	29	30
31	32	33	34	35	36	37	38	39	40
41	42	43	44	45	46	47	48	49	50
51	52	53	54	25	56	57	58	59	60
61	62	63	64	65	66	67	68	69	70
71	72	73	74	75	76	77	78	79	80
81	82	83	84	85	86	87	88	89	90
91	92	93	94	95	96	97	98	99	100

Award Certificate

Hot Math Topics

SUPER SOLVER

this certifies that

_____

has been awarded the Hot Math Topics Super Solver Certificate for

Excellence in Problem Solving

_____   _____
date   signature

Problems
and Tasks

Trace your baby finger.

Find something longer than your baby finger. Draw it.

Find something shorter than your baby finger. Draw it.

- -

Tell the location of three things in your classroom.

Use these words:

- on top of
- under
- inside of

Copy the animal onto the other grid.

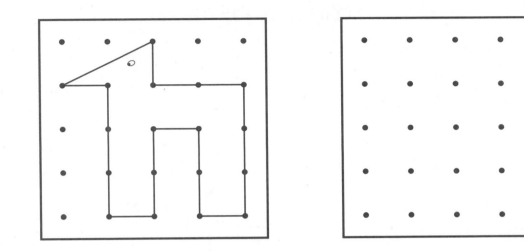

Play with a friend.

Make this pattern with tiles.

Close your eyes.

Have your friend take away a tile.

Open your eyes.

Guess the missing color.

Take turns.

red	blue	red
blue	red	blue
red	blue	red

Tell how B is different from A.

Tell how C is different from A.

Tell how D is different from A.

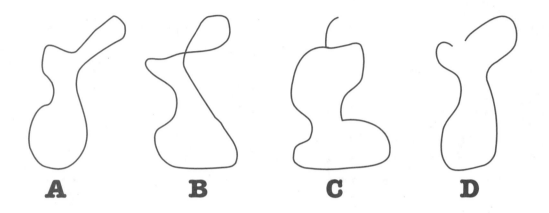

A   B   C   D

- -

Which piece will fit in the middle of the puzzle?

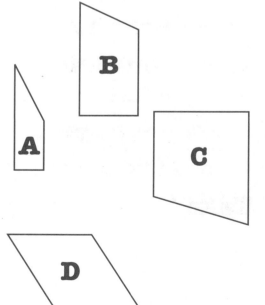

Puzzle

©Addison Wesley Longman, Inc./Published by Dale Seymour Publications®

I am a flat shape.

I have 4 sides.

Draw me.

How many corners do I have?

8

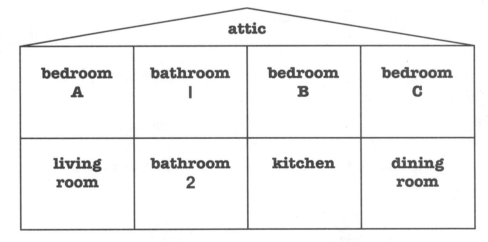

Bedroom B is above the kitchen.

Write 3 other things about the location of the rooms.

Use the words *above*, *below*, *next to*, or *between*.

The ladybug is | centimeter long.
How long is the worm?

- -

You need these blocks:

cube   rectangular   sphere   cylinder
          prism

Work with a friend. Take turns.
Close your eyes.
Have your friend hand you a block.
Guess the shape. Look to check.

©Addison Wesley Longman, Inc./Published by Dale Seymour Publications®

©Addison Wesley Longman, Inc./Published by Dale Seymour Publications®

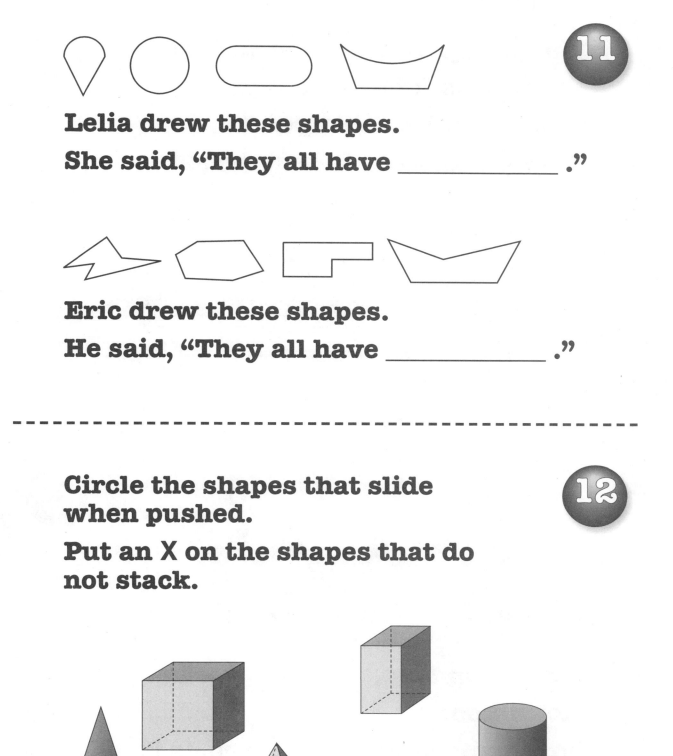

11

Lelia drew these shapes.

She said, "They all have _____ ."

Eric drew these shapes.

He said, "They all have _____ ."

- -

12

Circle the shapes that slide
when pushed.

Put an X on the shapes that do
not stack.

©Addison Wesley Longman, Inc./Published by Dale Seymour Publications®

Find things in the room that are

1. about as long as this pencil.

2. shorter than this pencil.

3. longer than 2 of these pencils.

13

- -

14

Pick a window.

Pick a door.

How many steps, heel to toe, is it from the window to the door?

Estimate.

Walk to check.

©Addison Wesley Longman, Inc./Published by Dale Seymour Publications®

What shape is number 15?
Tell how you know.

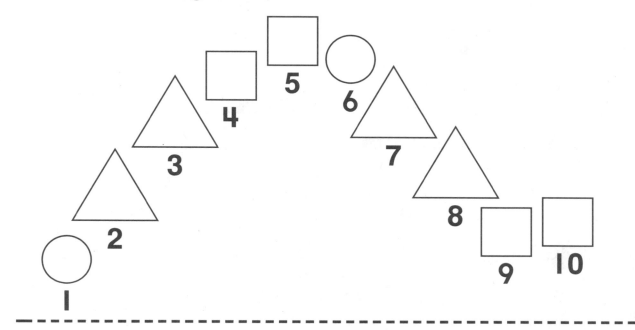

- -

Work with a friend.

Each of you get 5 interlocking cubes.

Make a shape like this one.

Have your friend copy it.

Take turns.

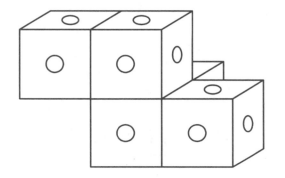

©Addison Wesley Longman, Inc./Published by Dale Seymour Publications®

17

Find things in the classroom.

Fill in the blanks.

The _____ is between the
_____ and the _____ .

The _____ is above the _____ .

The _____ is below the _____ .

- -

Make up a rule.

18

**Put an X on each shape that fits
the rule.**

Ask a friend to guess the rule.

©Addison Wesley Longman, Inc./Published by Dale Seymour Publications®

Fold a piece of paper in half.

Cut along the fold line.

Fold the 2 pieces in half.

Cut along the fold lines.

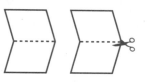

Use all 4 pieces.

Make the longest rectangle you can.

- -

Find the pairs of pieces that fit together.

Draw lines to show the matches.

Megan is the fourth child in line.
She is in the middle of the line.
Draw the rest of the children.
Draw a ring around Megan.

- -

Upside down,

looks like [   ] .

Draw each shape upside down.

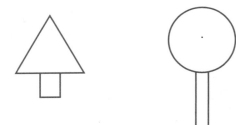

Find the 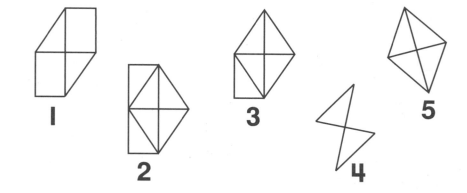 in each design.

Trace it in red.

1   2   3   4   5

- -

What do you know about squares?

Make a list.

Compare your list with a friend's list.

Draw a line in each shape.

Make 2 parts that are the same size and shape.

- -

Finish the drawing.

Draw

- a fish in the water

- a turtle on the rock

- a snake in front of the rock

- a squirrel to the right of the tree

- yourself in front of the tree

Go on a shape hunt.

Find 10 things shaped like a .

Make drawings of what you find.

Get a spoon, a paper cup, and some beans.

How many spoonfuls of beans will it take to fill the cup?

Estimate.

Fill the cup to check.

Use triangles and squares.

Draw a pattern.

Tell a friend how to make it.

Have your friend try to make it.

Do your patterns match?

- -

Put the straws in order from shortest to longest.

B ▨

C ▨▨▨▨▨▨▨▨

D ▨

A ▨▨▨

Write the letters.

_____   _____   _____   _____

shortest   longest

You need

- 2 red rods
- 2 white rods
- 1 purple rod
- 1 yellow rod

Use each rod.

Fill the space in the frame.

Trace the rods.

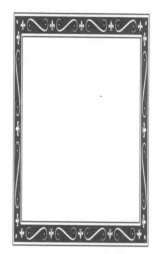

Connect dots to make triangles.

Do not use a dot more than once.

Do not cross lines.

How many different triangles can you make?

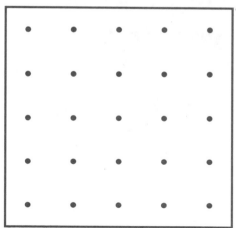

Get .

Each cone has chocolate, vanilla, and strawberry ice cream.

Color to show the different ways to have the ice cream.

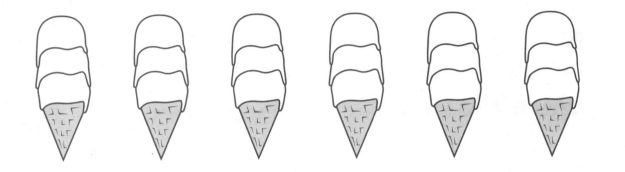

Work with a friend.

Start at the school.

Pick a place.

Tell your friend how to get there.

Did your friend find the place?

Take turns.

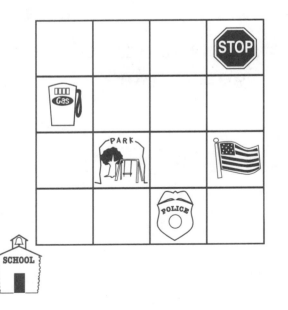

©Addison Wesley Longman, Inc./Published by Dale Seymour Publications®

35

Write a story about the picture.
Use these words:

above   below   inside

outside   between

- -

How many pieces of
will you need to make this?

36

How did you find out?

The lines show where to fold the designs.

Which designs have matching parts?

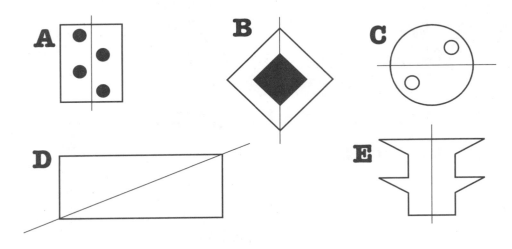

- -

Draw 4 things that roll.

Talk with a friend about the patterns you see.

Draw what you think comes next.

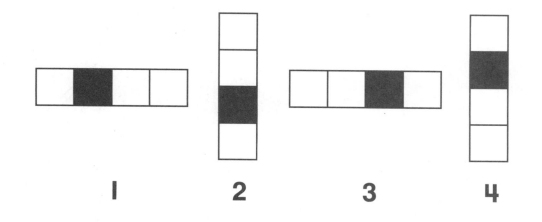

1   2   3   4

- -

Who won the race?

Clues

- Jan finished before Luis.
- Margo finished after Jan but before Luis.
- Jan finished after Ali.

Name each runner.

_____ _____ _____ _____

first   second   third   fourth

41

Get some pattern blocks.

What is the smallest number of blocks you need to fill this space?

Trace to show the blocks.

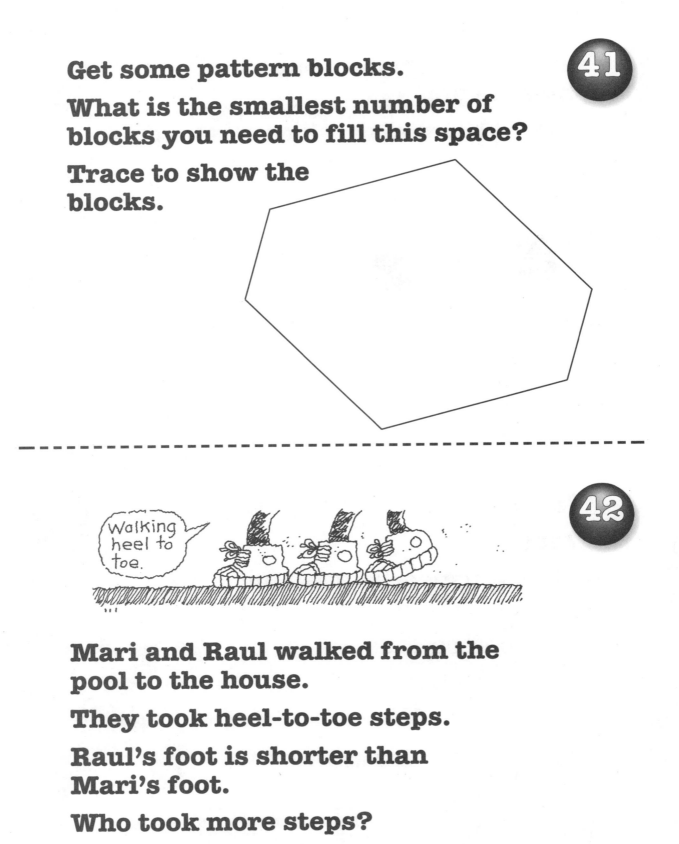

42

Walking heel to toe.

Mari and Raul walked from the pool to the house.

They took heel-to-toe steps.

Raul's foot is shorter than Mari's foot.

Who took more steps?

How do you know?

©Addison Wesley Longman, Inc./Published by Dale Seymour Publications®

©Addison Wesley Longman, Inc./Published by Dale Seymour Publications®

Which is bigger, Y or Z?
Tell what you did to find out.

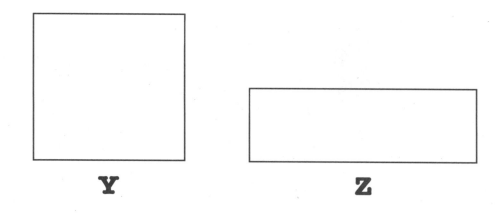

Y   Z

- -

Use the clues to find the card.

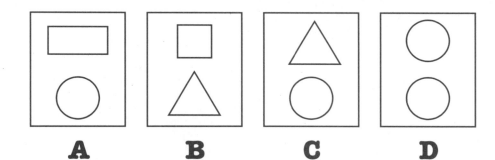

A   B   C   D

Clues

- There is a circle on the card.
- One of the shapes is not a circle.
- One of the shapes has 4 corners.

Which shape doesn't belong? Tell why.

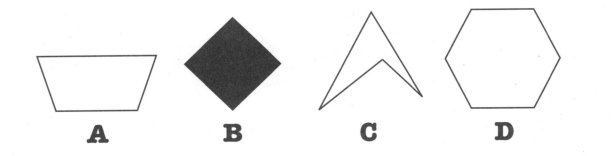

A   B   C   D

- -

How could you find out which holds more water, A or B?

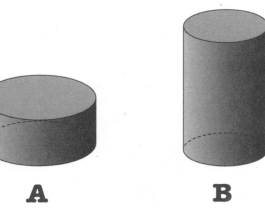

A   B

©Addison Wesley Longman, Inc./Published by Dale Seymour Publications®

©Addison Wesley Longman, Inc./Published by Dale Seymour Publications®

How many crayons long is your arm?

Write your estimate. _____

Use crayons to measure.

Write the number of crayons. _____

- -

Who will color more of the paper?

Tell how you know.

I will color 10 of these squares.

LANA

I will color 10 of these squares.

MARIA

Find things in your classroom that are shaped like a rectangular prism.

Make a list of what you find.

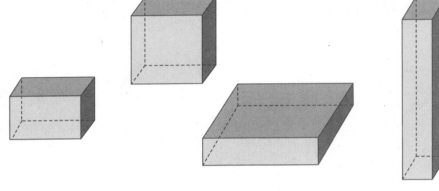

Rectangular prisms

©Addison Wesley Longman, Inc./Published by Dale Seymour Publications®

- -

How many rectangles do you see?

Look carefully.

Some are hidden!

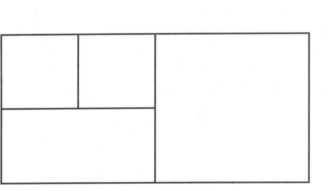

©Addison Wesley Longman, Inc./Published by Dale Seymour Publications®

Who lives farther from the park, Linda or Everett?

How did you decide?

You want to make building A look like building B.

How many more small cubes will you need?

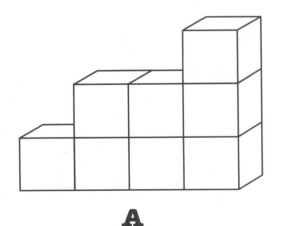

A

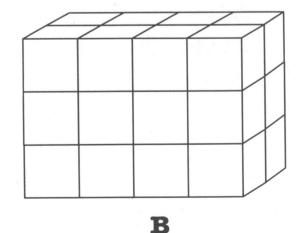

B

Get a geoboard.

53

Make a 4-sided shape with all sides equal. Draw it.

Make a 4-sided shape with only 2 sides equal. Draw it.

Compare your shapes with a friend's shapes.

54

Get a triangle, a square, and a circle.

Put them in a row.

Draw them.

Change the order.

Draw them again.

How many different orders can you find?

Ask a friend to get dot paper.

Tell your friend how to draw this shape.

Don't show your friend this shape.

Is your friend's shape just like this one?

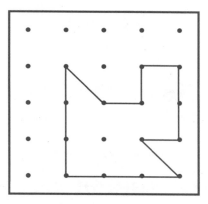

Get a cup and a piece of paper.

Trace around the bottom of the cup.

Cut out the circle.

Fold it in half.

Now fold it in half the other way.

Open the paper.

Connect the points on the edges.

Tell about the shape you made.

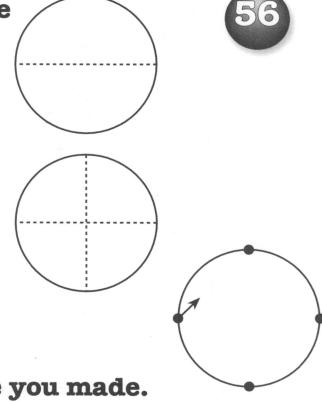

Use 6 toothpicks. Make 2 triangles. Draw the triangles.

Use 5 toothpicks. Make 2 triangles. Draw the triangles.

- -

Follow the clues to color the train cars.

Clues

- The engine is the first car. It is red.

- The fourth car is blue.

- The sixth car is green.

- The car between the fourth car and the sixth car is yellow.

- Color the other cars orange.

©Addison Wesley Longman, Inc./Published by Dale Seymour Publications®

With 3 tiles you can make these:

Tiles must share sides.

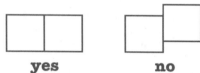

yes   no

**Draw shapes you can make with
4 tiles.**

- -

©Addison Wesley Longman, Inc./Published by Dale Seymour Publications®

Cut each rectangle in half.
Draw lines to show the cuts.
**Show 4 different ways to make
the cuts.**

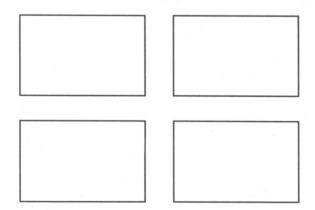

©Addison Wesley Longman, Inc./Published by Dale Seymour Publications®

Use these tangram pieces.

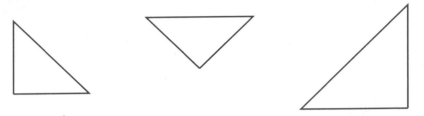

Make these shapes.
Trace to show the pieces.

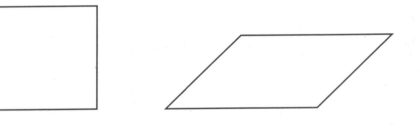

Which 2 puzzle pieces are the same?

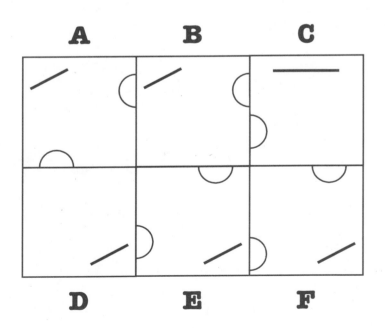

©Addison Wesley Longman, Inc./Published by Dale Seymour Publications®

Luke walks to school.

Write directions to help him.

Start at his house.

Stay on the sidewalks.

**Compare your directions
with a friend's directions.**

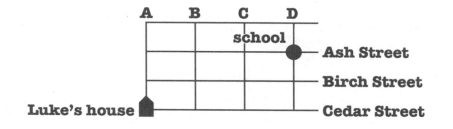

A   B   C   D

school   Ash Street

Birch Street

Luke's house   Cedar Street

63

- -

Draw these on the shelves:

64

- A is on the bottom shelf.

- A 🌱 is on the top shelf.

- A 📖 is on the shelf above
  the 🥫 .

- An 🍎 is on the shelf below
  the 🌱.

- A ☕ is between the 📖
  and the 🍎 .

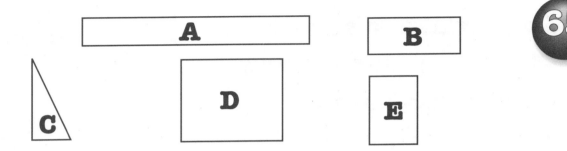

65

Which pieces fit together to make this shape?

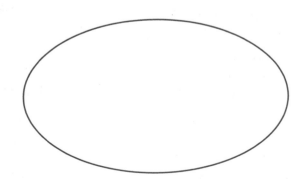

- -

66

How many **can fit inside the oval?**

Estimate.

Compare your estimate with a friend's estimate.

Use ⬯⬯⬯ **to check.**

©Addison Wesley Longman, Inc./Published by Dale Seymour Publications®

©Addison Wesley Longman, Inc./Published by Dale Seymour Publications®

Put a mirror on the design card.

Which one of the other designs can you make?

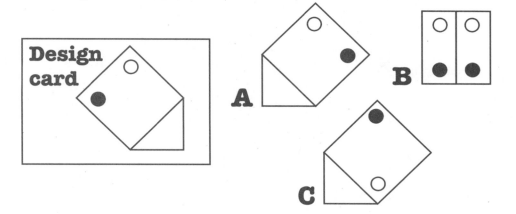

Draw 2 other designs you made with the mirror.

- -

Draw 2 lines in the first square.

Separate the square into 3 triangles.

Can you find another way?

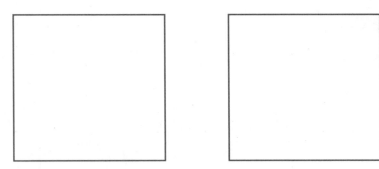

How many **will it take to cover the big square?**

Tell how you decided.

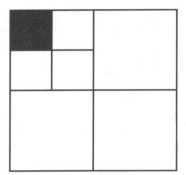

69

You and a friend each need

- a red block
- a blue block
- a yellow block
- a green block

Build a tower.

Tell your friend how to make it.

Are your towers the same?

Take turns.

70

Draw the circles in Row 6.

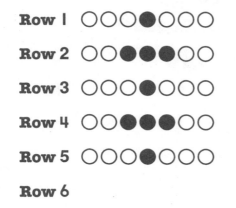

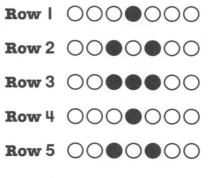

- -

Get some pattern blocks.
Can you fill the space using blocks of only one color?
What color?

Can you do it another way?
What color?

There are 4 children and 1 cake.

Cut the cake so each child gets a piece the same size and shape.

Cut the cake in another way.

©Addison Wesley Longman, Inc./Published by Dale Seymour Publications®

Mara is standing in line.

Four children are in front of me. Ten children are in line.

©Addison Wesley Longman, Inc./Published by Dale Seymour Publications®

How many children are behind Mara?

Tell how you know.

How many triangles can you find?
Look carefully.
Some are hidden!

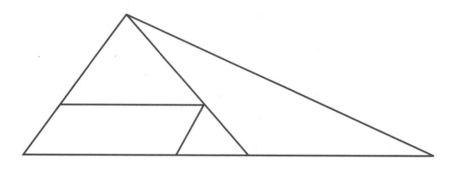

- -

Clues

- Lelia lives 2 floors above Julian.
- Jon lives on the top floor.
- Petra lives above Julian.
- Lonnie lives on the floor between Jon and Lelia.
- Cora lives on the first floor.

Write the correct name next to each floor.

Julian lives on the second floor.

sixth	_____
fifth	_____
fourth	_____
third	_____
second	Julian
first	_____

Name the letter of the block.

- to the right of a B: _____
- between a B and a Y: _____
- 2 blocks below the top R: _____
- to the left of a G: _____

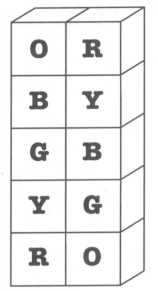

O	R
B	Y
G	B
Y	G
R	O

Walking heel to toe.

The children walked heel-to-toe across the room.

- Barry took 50 steps.
- Alan took 45 steps.
- Dana took 30 steps.

Who has the longest foot?

How do you know?

Bottom of the block:

Top of the block:

Which block is it?

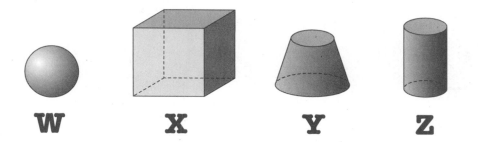

W   **X**   **Y**   **Z**

Tell why Y is not the block.

- -

The car is at K.

L is 3 blocks from K.

Where else could the car go that is 3 blocks from K?

Mark other points that are 3 blocks from K.

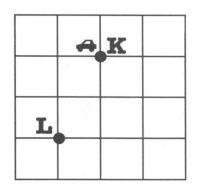

What am I?

- I have four sides.
- I am not a square.
- I am not a rectangle.
- My sides are not all the same length.

Draw me.

Complete the tile that comes next in the pattern.

Tell how you know.

©Addison Wesley Longman, Inc./Published by Dale Seymour Publications®

I put 4 marbles in the tube.

- Black was first.
- Red was second.
- White was third.
- Yellow was fourth.

I tipped the tube.

Which color came out first?

Which color came out last?

83

Kara is holding Jin Lee's left hand.

Kara is holding Lisa's right hand.

Write the names.

84

_____   _____   _____

Take away
3 toothpicks to
get 1 triangle.

Take away
2 toothpicks to
get 3 triangles.

85

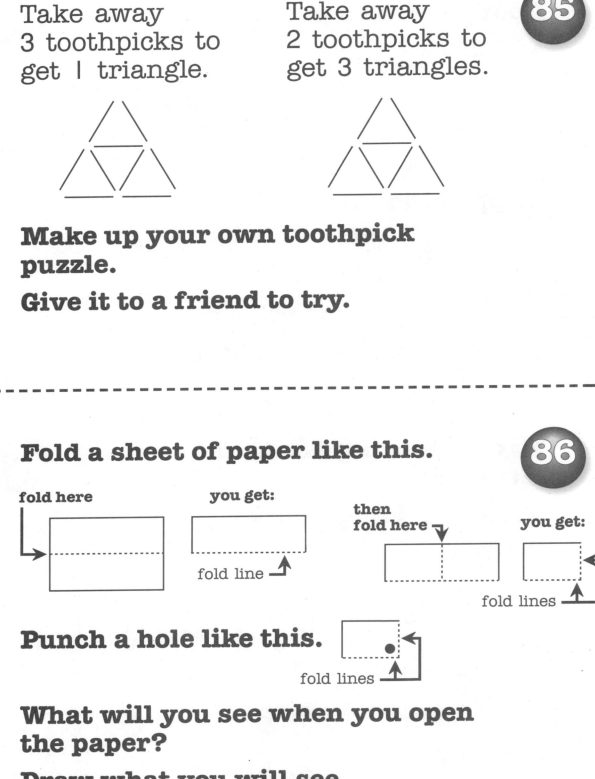

Make up your own toothpick puzzle.

Give it to a friend to try.

- -

Fold a sheet of paper like this.

86

fold here

you get:

fold line

then
fold here

you get:

fold lines

Punch a hole like this.

fold lines

What will you see when you open the paper?

Draw what you will see.

Open the paper to check your drawing.

©Addison Wesley Longman, Inc./Published by Dale Seymour Publications®

These rods are in order from shortest to longest.

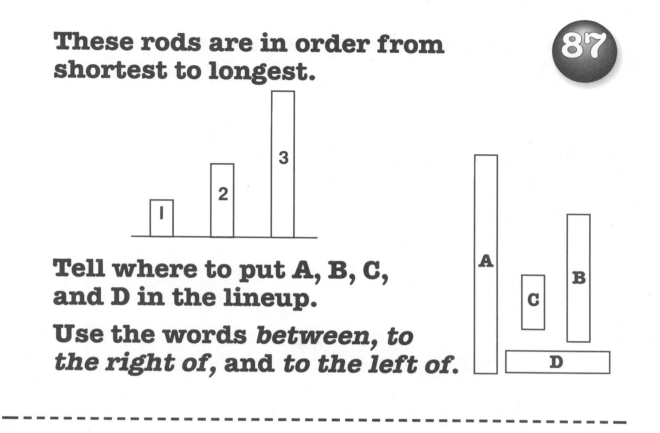

Tell where to put A, B, C, and D in the lineup.

Use the words *between*, *to the right of*, and *to the left of*.

- -

A cube has 6 faces.

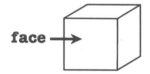

face →

Look at buildings A, B, and C.

In each building, how many outside faces do not touch the table?

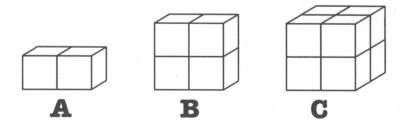

A   B   C

87

88

Put the cookies on the tray to bake.

Use all 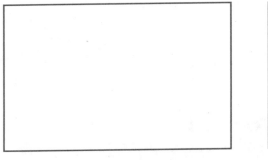 or all 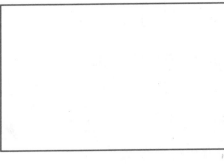.

Would 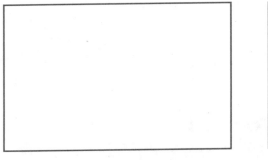 cookies or 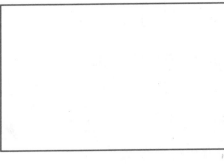 cookies give you more to eat?

89

Name the letter in

90

- the bottom row, column 3: _____

- the top row, middle column: _____

- the middle row, middle column: _____

- column 1, row 3: _____

Make up a grid of letters.

Tell the position of 4 letters.

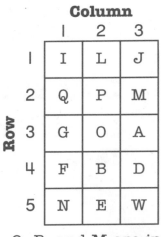

Column

	1	2	3
1	I	L	J
2	Q	P	M
3	G	O	A
4	F	B	D
5	N	E	W

Q, P, and M are in row 2.

J, M, A, D, and W are in column 3.

How many blocks do you need to build this tower?

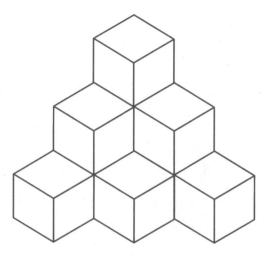

Which is greater, the height or the width?

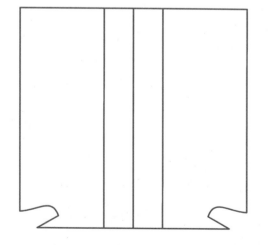

Guess first. Then check.

Pick one place.

What are some shapes you might see?

93

- -

Get some blocks.

Build a wall on a side of this rectangle.

94

Estimate. How many blocks will it take to build a wall around the whole rectangle?

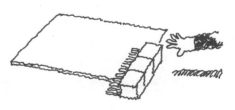

Build the wall to check.

Make squares from squares.

Use graph paper.

Square 1

1 small square

Square 2

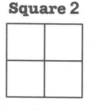

4 small squares

Square 3

9 small squares

How many small squares does square 4 have?

How many small squares does square 5 have?

- -

Connect the dots.

How many different size squares can you make?

Work with a friend.

How many hidden faces are there for 5 cubes?

How many for 6 cubes?

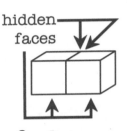 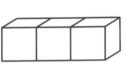 

hidden face

hidden faces

1 cube **1 hidden face**	**2 cubes** **4 hidden faces**	**3 cubes** **7 hidden faces**	**4 cubes** **10 hidden faces**

- -

Which line is the longest?

98

Guess first. Then use paper clips to measure. Write numbers in the boxes.

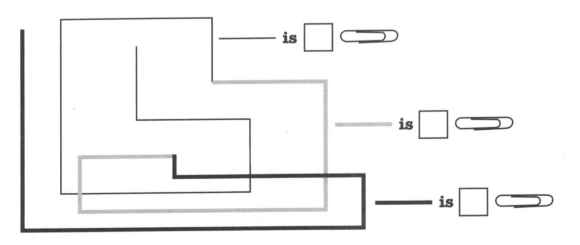

is [ ]

is [ ]

is [ ]

Did you guess right?

©Addison Wesley Longman, Inc./Published by Dale Seymour Publications®

This card is red on one side and blue on the other side.

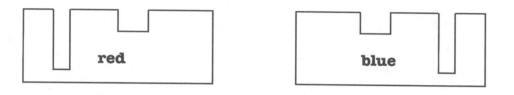

red   blue

Tell what color is showing.
Write *red* or *blue* on each card.

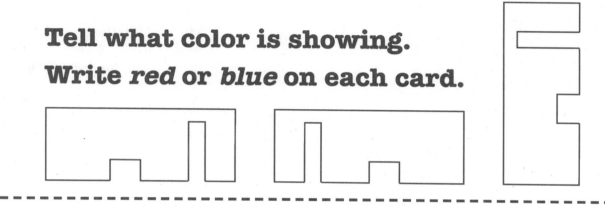

- -

Finish the pattern.
Fill in the designs.

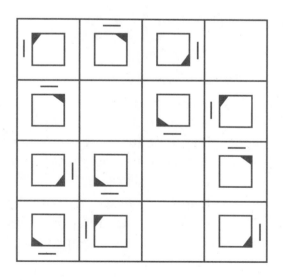

Answers

1. Drawings will vary.

2. Answers will vary.

3. The animals should be identical.

5. B crosses over itself. C has a tail. D is not closed.

6. piece B

7. Drawings will vary; all should have 4 corners.

8. Answers will vary.

9. about 6 cm

11. curves; straight sides

12. The cone, sphere, and pyramid should have an X; all but the sphere should be circled.

13. Answers will vary.

14. Answers will vary.

15. ☐ ; Explanations will vary.

17. Answers will vary.

18. Rules will vary.

19. ☐☐☐☐☐

20. Lines should connect the two quadrilaterals, the triangle and the pentagon, and the two curved pieces.

21. Drawings should show 7 children in line with a ring around the fourth child.

22.

23. Children should have traced the 4 in each design.

24. Lists will vary.

25. The equilateral triangle can be bisected three ways; the circle can be bisected by any diameter.

26. Drawings should show a fish in the water, a turtle on the rock, a snake in front of the rock, a squirrel to the right of the tree, and the child in front of the tree.

27. Drawings will vary.

28. Answers will vary.

29. Patterns and answers will vary.

30. B, D, A, C

31. Answers will vary.

32. Answers will vary. Possible answer: 5 triangles

33. C, V, S   C, S, V   V, S, C   V, C, S   S, V, C   S, C, V

35. Stories will vary.

36. 4; Explanations will vary. One possibility is to cut a piece of paper the length of the short line segment and use it to mark off segments on the other shape.

37. B and E (Note: If children look for identical parts rather than mirror images, they might answer A, B, C, and D.)

38. Drawings will vary.

39. Possible answer: ;
Answers will depend on the pattern identified.

40. Ali, Jan, Margo, Luis

41. 4 blocks;

42. Raul. Since his foot is shorter, he took more steps.

43. Y is bigger. Possible explanation: Cut Z apart to try to cover Y.

44. A

45. Possible answers: B doesn't belong because it is shaded. C doesn't belong because it is caved in. D doesn't belong because it doesn't have 4 sides.

46. Possible answer: Fill A. Pour it into B. If it doesn't fill B, then A holds less water. If it overflows B, then A holds more water.

47. Answers will vary.

48. Lana; Each of Lana's squares is larger than each of Maria's squares.

49. Possible answer: books, blocks, and boxes

50. There are 7 rectangles in all.

51. Linda lives farther from the park. Explanations will vary.

52. B has 24 small cubes; A has 8 small cubes. You will need 16 small cubes to make A look like B. (Note: If children recognize that 1 or 2 cubes might be "hidden" behind other cubes in A, their answers would be 15 and 14, respectively.)

53. Shapes will vary.

54. There are 6 orders:

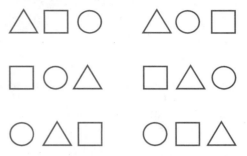

56. The shape has 4 sides and 4 angles. All sides are the same length. All angles are the same. The shape is a square.

57.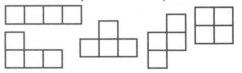

58. from engine: red, orange, orange, blue, yellow, green

59. There are 5 possible shapes :

60. Possible answer:

61.

62. A and E

63. Possible answer: Luke leaves home. He walks up A Street to Ash. He turns right and walks to D Street. The school is on the corner of D and Ash streets.

64. Drawings should show a flowerpot on the top shelf; a book and an apple on the middle shelf with a cup between them, and a can on the bottom shelf.

65. A and D

66. Estimates and answers will vary.

67. A and B; Designs will vary.

68. Answers will vary. Possible answer:

69. 16; Explanations will vary.

71. Row 6 OOO●●OO   Row 6 OOO●●OO

72. Green and red pattern blocks will work.

73. Some possible answers:

74. 5 children are behind Mara; Explanations will vary.

75. There are 5 triangles in all.

76. From top to bottom, the names are Jon, Lonnie, Lelia, Petra, Julian, and Cora.

77. Y, G, B, Y

78. Dana has the longest foot. He took the fewest steps.

79. Z; Y is incorrect because the top and bottom are different-size circles.

80.

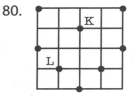

81. Answers will vary. Some possibilities:

82.  ; Explanations will vary.

83. Yellow came out first; black came out last.

84. Jin Lee, Kara, Lisa

85.

Puzzles will vary.

86.

87. Possible answer: Put C between 1 and 2, D and then B between 2 and 3, and A to the right of 3.

88. A, 8 faces; B, 14 faces; C, 20 faces

89. Square cookies would give more to eat, as there would be less empty space on the tray.

90. W, L, O, G; Grids will vary.

91. 10 blocks

92. They are the same length.

93. Answers will vary.

94. Answers will vary.

95. Square 4 has 16 small squares; square 5 has 25 small squares.

96. Six sizes are possible:

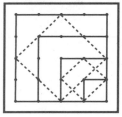

97. 5 cubes, 13 hidden faces; 6 cubes, 16 hidden faces

98. The thin black line is the longest. Numbers will vary depending on the size of paper clips used.

99. red; blue; red

100.

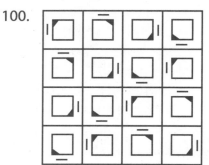